HARLEY QUINN

The Clown Princess of Crime

STEVE KORTÉ

RP Minis®
Hachette Book Group
1290 Avenue of the Americas, New York, NY 10104
www.runningpress.com
@Running_Press

First Edition: July 2021

Published by RP Minis, an imprint of Perseus Books, LLC, a subsidiary of Hachette Book Group, Inc. The RP Minis name and logo is a trademark of the Hachette Book Group.

ISBN: 978-0-7624-7568-4

CONTENTS

HARLEY
QUINN

INTRODUCTION

What kind of woman would be drawn to a super-villain like The Joker? For Harleen Quinzel, it was love at first sight when she met the Clown Prince of Crime. Unfortunately for Harleen, her attraction to The Joker drove her completely insane and inspired her to adopt a new identity. She donned a harlequin's costume, smeared white makeup on her face, and embarked on a new life as Harley Quinn, the

Clown Princess of Crime. She then teamed up with The Joker to become his prankster partner-in-crime.

Harley had a unique personality that was both lovable and lethal, and it soon became clear that she was destined for a bigger role than serving as The Joker's girlfriend. So she branched out and went solo. She also joined a few teams, including the Suicide Squad, the Gotham City Sirens, and the Birds of Prey. After taking animation, video games, and comic books by storm, Harley went Hollywood and stole scenes in several live-action feature films.

Along the way, Harley's cheerfully unhinged sense of humor and total lack of impulse control have won her fans in every form of media she has invaded.

SIGH
Love's Wacky Fury

AN ANIMATED DEBUT

When *Batman: The Animated Series* premiered on TV in the fall of 1992, it won critical acclaim for its exciting stories and striking character designs. Many fans thought it was the best Batman media adaptation they had ever seen. It was also an instant ratings success. Most of the episodes featured famous villains from the Dark Knight's longstanding Rogues Gallery, but a few new foes appeared as well. One of those

Joker's accomplice in the episode "Joker's Favor." With her madcap personality and her wisecracking voice right out of Brooklyn, New York, Harley was a scene stealer right from the start.

"I needed a gang for The Joker to interact with," recalled Dini. "And I thought, what if I shake it up a little bit? In the '60s show, there would sometimes be a random female henchperson thrown in with the group, so I thought, let's try putting in something like that. And I thought, what if the girl, instead of just taking orders, is also really upbeat and fun, and playfully wicked. I thought that would be a real contrast to The Joker, instead of someone who's just following orders or scared of him."

Bruce Timm designed a character with her face covered in white paint, and gave her a formfitting red-and-black harlequin costume,

ZOK!
NEWSS

complete with jingling bells at the tips of her cap. Actress Arleen Sorkin, a friend of Dini's, was another inspiration for the character. Sorkin would provide Harley's voice for many years.

Harley was originally intended as a throwaway character, but she quickly became a favorite of viewers and the show's creators. She also began her long-running and mostly unrequited romantic relationship with The Joker. Dini adds, "One way we humanized the least human of Batman's enemies was to put him in a relationship with a woman who, for whatever reasons, adores him."

Harley's popularity grew so fast that she became the central focus of several subsequent episodes. As Dini explained, "Eventually each of the show's directors wanted to do a Harley episode, so the character began to appear in stories without The Joker," said Dini.

After conquering the world of TV animation, Harley quickly migrated to print. She made her comic book debut in 1993 in *The Batman Adventures*, a new title inspired by the animated series. She then won even greater fame in the 64-page graphic novel *The Batman Adventures: Mad Love*. That 1994 comic book, written by Paul Dini and illustrated by Bruce Timm, presented a new origin story for Harley.

In this story she was Harleen Quinzel, a psychiatrist who had

DC
PSYCHOTIC, MASS-MURDERING CLOWNS
AND THE WOMEN WHO LOVE THEM.
THE BATMAN ADVENTURES
"MAD LOVE"

graduated at the top of her class from Gotham University. She began her psychiatric residency at a prominent hospital and soon found herself drawn to the study of the criminal mind. She moved her practice to Arkham Asylum and started conducting private sessions with The Joker. She found him to be as charming as he was insane, and she soon fell madly in love with him. Harleen's love for The Joker was so intense that she transformed herself into Harley Quinn and decided to follow in his demented footsteps.

In order to prove her devotion to The Joker, she set a deathtrap to kill Batman. Surprisingly, The Joker was furious with Harley when he found out about her plans . . . but only because he had been left out of the fun.

Readers loved this new version of Harley, and *Mad Love* won the comic industry's Eisner Award for the best single issue of 1994. With praise from fans and critics, not to mention an Eisner Award, is it any surprise that Harley next set her sights on the "real" DC universe?

HARLEY GETS REAL

In 1999, Harley underwent yet another personality change and invaded the “real” DC universe. In *Batman: Harley Quinn*, writer Paul Dini and artist Yvel Guichet guided her into a more realistic world, one that was definitely grittier and more violent than her previous animated realm. Dini also altered aspects of Harley’s past, making her an intern at Arkham who was locked up in her own cell after she freed The Joker.

You can't keep a good (or bad) character down, though, and in 2000 Harley began her own monthly comic book series that ran for thirty-eight issues. Stepping out from the shadow of The Joker, Harley interacted with dozens of Batman's most famous villains in her new series. She even made her first leap into live-action on the 2002 television series *Birds of Prey*. Actress Mia Sara portrayed Harleen Quinzel, a psychiatrist with a few psychoses of her own. On the show, Quinzel battled the Huntress, Black

Canary, and Oracle—who previously fought crime as Batgirl.

As the decade wore on, Harley mostly fought Batman and continued her dysfunctional infatuation with her "Puddin'," as she lovingly nicknamed The Joker. It was truly a love-hate relationship, with their affections for each other shifting from issue to issue. Whenever Batman appeared, however, Harley was fiercely protective of The Joker. She would declare, "Back off, B-Man! You want Mister J, you gotta go through me!"

Harley also teamed up with Poison Ivy several times and played a pivotal role in the "Hush" storyline. She even found time to join the Secret Society of Super-Villains, the Secret Six, and the Gotham City Sirens. That last group was a villainous threesome that included Catwoman and Poison Ivy.

The year 2007 almost saw the demise of Harley in a shocking story in *Batman* #663, written by Grant Morrison and drawn by John VanFleet. It presented The Joker at his psychotic worst as he enlisted Harley in a plot to murder all of his past henchmen. What Harley did not know was that The Joker even planned to murder her! To foil his plan, the ever-resourceful Harley shot her beloved Joker in the shoulder.

HAHA

HARLEY REBORN

The year 2011 was another big one for Harley. First, she appeared in the video game *Batman: Arkham Asylum*. And in the pages of DC's comics, she got a major makeover. Harley ditched her jester's outfit for a sleeveless top, tight shorts, and boots. She now sported a two-tone hairstyle that was half red and half black, and she also acquired a permanent chalky-white skin color, the result of The Joker pushing her into a vat of acid!

She joined yet another team when government agent Amanda Waller inducted Harley into Task Force X, also known as the Suicide Squad, a covert strike force made up of super-villains. Harley thrived in her new role as she found herself working alongside some of the world's most ruthless criminals.

"How cool would it be to have my own comic book?" pondered Harley in the opening pages of *Harley Quinn* #0, the first issue of her new solo comic book that was released in 2013. Refusing, as usual, to play by the rules, Harley routinely broke the fourth wall and chatted with the two writers of her new title (Jimmy Palmiotti and Amanda Conner) and commented on the nineteen artists that illustrated the issue.

In 2016, Harley leapt into *another* medium, making her feature film debut in the live-action *Suicide Squad* movie. Actress Margot Robbie portrayed the Clown Princess of Crime, and many people thought that Harley stole the movie.

HYENAS
SOCIETY
HARLEY

That same year, DC relaunched its entire line of ongoing comics in an event known as "Rebirth," and Harley changed yet again. She acquired a new comic book series, revised her costume, and returned to her blonde hairstyle, with the tips of her hair tinted blue and pink. Harley was now located in New York's Coney Island, where she became a protector of her new neighborhood.

Palmiotti explained, "We understand that she is a bad guy in general but a good person at heart and try to keep a delicate balance between the two. With that, we took the girl out of Gotham, and worked on building up a new supporting cast and focused mainly on developing a personality that we felt would be the right tone for a character that lived through The Joker and Suicide Squad and is now in a place where she is her own woman, in control of her own life."

As Harley's popularity continued to grow, she inspired more creators—including writers, artists, and filmmakers—to launch a wave

of projects starring her. There were new comic book series, including *Harley Quinn & Poison Ivy*, *Harleen*, *Harley Quinn and the Birds of Prey*, and more. She even managed to star in a movie or two and wedged her name into the title of the 2020 film *Birds of Prey (and the Fantabulous Emancipation of One Harley Quinn)*.

CONCLUSION

In her relatively short lifetime, Harley Quinn has become a true multimedia superstar. If a new medium is ever invented, there is little doubt that she will conquer it.

From Harley's humble beginning as a lovesick sidekick, she has evolved into one of the most popular characters in the DC universe. Harley has truly won the last laugh.

Or, as she once said to The Joker, "It is to laugh, huh Mistah J?"

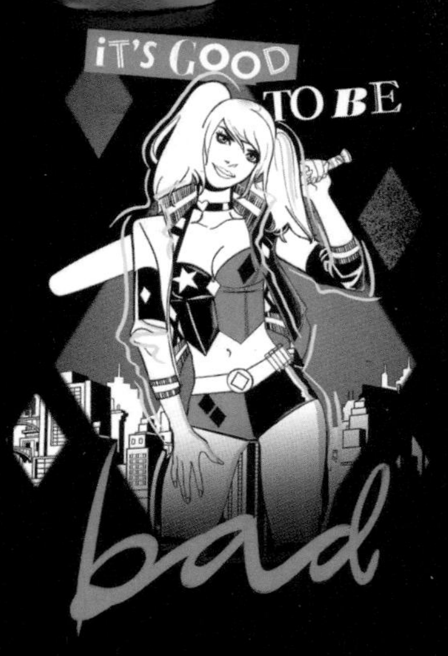
iT'S GOOD
TO BE
bad

This book has been bound using handcraft methods and Smyth-sewn to ensure durability.

Designed by Josh McDonnell.

Written by Steve Korté.